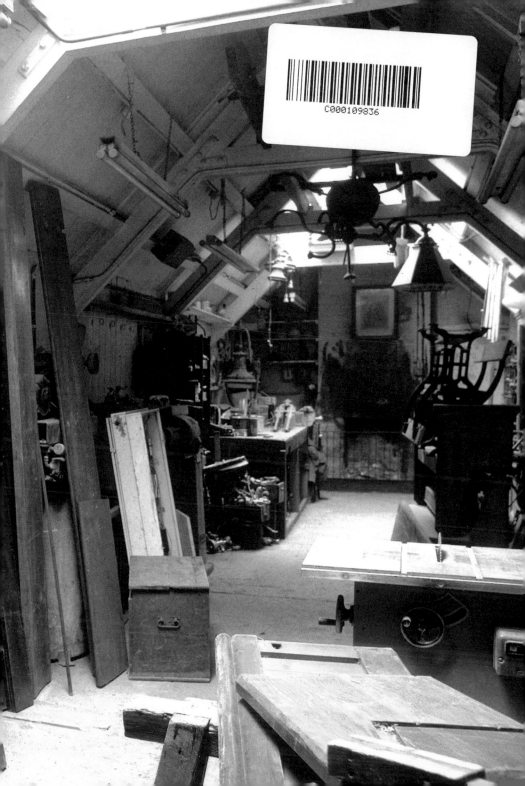

Made Simple

WOODWORKING
JOINTS

David Holloway

Made Simple

WOODWORKING

JOINTS

David Holloway

Bloomsbury Books
London

Made Simple
WOODWORKING
JOINTS

Page 2: Soundly made woodworking joints are the foundation of our favourite things.

This edition published in 1994 by Bloomsbury Books,

an imprint of The Godfrey Cave Group,

42 Bloomsbury Street, London. WC1B 3QJ

Under license from Harlaxton Publishing Limited

2 Avenue Road, Grantham, Lincolnshire, NG31 6TA, United Kingdom.

A member of the Weldon International Group of Companies.

Publisher: Robin Burgess

Design and Coordination: Rachel Rush

Editing: Martyn Hocking

Illustrator: David Cook, Linden Artists

Photography: Chris Allen, Forum Advertising Limited

Typesetting: Seller's, Grantham

Colour Reproduction: GA Graphics, Stamford

Printing: Imago, Singapore

British Library Cataloguing-in-Publication data.

A catalogue record for this book is available from the British Library.

Title: Made Simple - WOODWORKING JOINTS

ISBN: 1-85471-377-9

CONTENTS

ABOVE: The potential of timber is limited only by the confines of our imagination.

The ability to make woodworking joints accurately and neatly marks the difference between a real do-it-yourselfer and a bodger.

Few jobs require the skill and expertise needed to make a mitred dovetail joint or a stopped housing, but many require a simple butt joint or a lapped joint to join timber end to end or at right angles.

An understanding of woodworking joints – how they are made and what they are used for – allows the do-it-yourselfer to cope with existing joints which have failed in one way or another – on furniture, on windows and doors, on drawers, on picture frames, on kitchen units, on bookcases, on skirting boards, on beds and on frameworks around the house.

The biggest change in woodworking over recent years has been the introduction of man-made boards – particularly chipboard, blockboard and, more recently, medium-density fibreboard (MDF). The development of techniques for covering these boards with either an easy-to-clean melamine finish or a thin layer of real wood veneer has allowed shelving and furniture to be built at a fraction of the cost of using real wood but with an appearance which is both aesthetically pleasing and easy to finish and keep looking good.

Along with these materials has come a new selection of jointing methods, especially the use of so-called 'knock-down' fittings widely used on, for example, kitchen units. These have done away with the need to employ traditional jointing methods and many of these fittings can often be used in place of traditional joints when working with real wood.

Few special tools are needed for making woodworking joints, whether traditional ones or modern 'knock-down' ones. What is needed, however, is the ability to mark out the wood or the board squarely and to cut it accurately. Various devices are at hand to help with both of these, but a good eye, sharp tools, attention to detail and a steady hand are all essentials. Unlike some other do-it-yourself skills, woodworking can be done slowly, constantly checking that you are 'on-line' and that everything is square, in line and the correct size.

When done properly, the results invariably justify the time and the effort.

Made Simple

BASIC MATERIALS

All natural timber is categorized under two heading – either softwood or hardwood.

Softwoods come from evergreen coniferous (cone-bearing) trees – pine, spruce and fir – whilst hardwoods come from deciduous, broad-leaved, trees – elm, oak and ash.

Softwoods are cheaper than hardwoods and are widely used in house building – for doors, windows, floorboards, joists, roof structures, partition walls and so on.

Hardwoods, which are more durable and generally more attractive, have traditionally been used for furniture and are finished by waxing, varnishing, staining and French polishing to preserve and enhance the natural appearance of the timber. Although more expensive than softwoods, they are increasingly used for doors, windows and their frames and for constructions such as conservatories.

BUYING TIMBER

The biggest problem in buying timber is understanding the sizing – the relationship between the European metric standard and the old imperial standard of measurement.

Although timber is, today, priced by the metre (or for bulk purchase by the 100m), it is actually sold in lengths which are multiples of 0.3m (300mm), which is nearly, but not quite, equal to the imperial foot – 300mm is actually 11.81in. This 'metric foot' may suit older carpenters, but can be a nightmare if you actually need a six foot length but are supplied with a length that is just over an inch less. If you are familiar only with the metric system and naturally used to dealing in multiples of 5 or 10, then the supply of multiples of 0.3m can still be confusing.

The sizing of timber becomes even more complicated when specifying widths and thicknesses. The direct conversion to metric sizes from the old imperial sizes has led to odd amounts such as 12mm/½in, 19mm/¾in, 22mm/⅞in, 38mm/1½in and so on, but most other sizes – 25mm, 50mm, 75mm, 100mm – are a little more intelligible because of the fortunate coincidence that 25mm is roughly one inch.

The real problem comes in the fact that wood is sold in two ways – 'sawn' and 'planed'.

SAWN TIMBER – has rough surfaces and it is the size it says it is – so 100mmx50mm sawn timber is actually 100mm wide by 50mm thick.

PLANED TIMBER – has smooth surfaces. It is described as 100mmx50mm, but is a finished size of 97mmx47mm, the missing 3mm being the amount taken off by the planing machine.

Sawn timber is used in basic house construction where it is out of sight – roofing timbers, floor and ceiling joists, stud partition walls and so on. Planed timber, usually known as PAR (planed all round) is used in exposed joinery – doors, windows and their frames, floorboards, shelving, cupboards and so on.

Timber is sold in builders merchants, do-it-yourself stores and at specialist timber merchants. The best selection and prices are generally obtainable at timber merchants – and there is an additional bonus in that the timber will be well seasoned and properly stored.

COMMON TIMBER WIDTHS

| 12 | 19 | 32 | 38 | 50 | 75 | 100 | 125 | 150 | 175 | 200 | 225 | mm |

| ½ | ¾ | 1¼ | 1½ | 2 | 3 | 4 | 5 | 6 | 7 | 8 | 9 | inch |

COMMON TIMBER THICKNESS

'Seasoning' (drying out) is important for timber. If you buy wood which has not been properly seasoned, it can warp or split once it has been used.

Recently, some of the larger do-it-yourself superstores have improved their sources of supply for timber and it is now possible to buy good timber in these large shops, which is convenient as you will probably be buying other supplies there at the same time.

When buying timber from any source, however, it is vital that you inspect it to make sure it is straight, true and free of faults, such as splits or dead knots. This applies particularly when you are having timber delivered by a timber merchant, when you should also check that you have got the lengths you asked for, if this is critical.

SOFTWOODS

The most common softwood available is pine or fir, sometimes simply known as 'deal' as it is generally sold in planks.

It varies in colour from yellow to brown but because of the size and shape of pine and fir trees, the maximum width generally available is 175mm/7in. For larger sizes – 225mm/9in and 300mm/12in – parana pine is available. This is a beautiful wood, with red streaks and an almost complete absence of knots, but it is two to four times the price of ordinary softwood.

A whiter coloured wood is spruce which, like pine and fir, has a wide variety of uses. A particular durable softwood is western red cedar and this is often used outside the home – for shingles, cladding, garden furniture and buildings such as greenhouses and sheds.

HARDWOODS

Over recent years, there has been increasing concern about the use of hardwoods, especially those from tropical rain forests.

However, many suppliers of hardwoods have a reforestation policy where one or more trees are planted for each one cut down. So, apart from the endangered species – rosewood, ebony, utile, affrormosia, mahogany, teak and obeche – you should not worry about using hardwoods.

Although real mahogany is an endangered species, there are many other woods (such as sapele) sold as 'mahogany' and this is still one of the most popular hardwoods – especially as a veneer – a thin sheet of one wood used to cover another. Mahogany has a warm reddish colour and a distinctive grain structure. Beech and ash are both straight-grained hardwoods and used for tool handles and furniture making. Oak is expensive, but is one of the most durable and hardest to work, of all timbers. Ramin, a hard, light-coloured hardwood, is commonly sold in mouldings and thin sections and used as a 'lipping' on other materials.

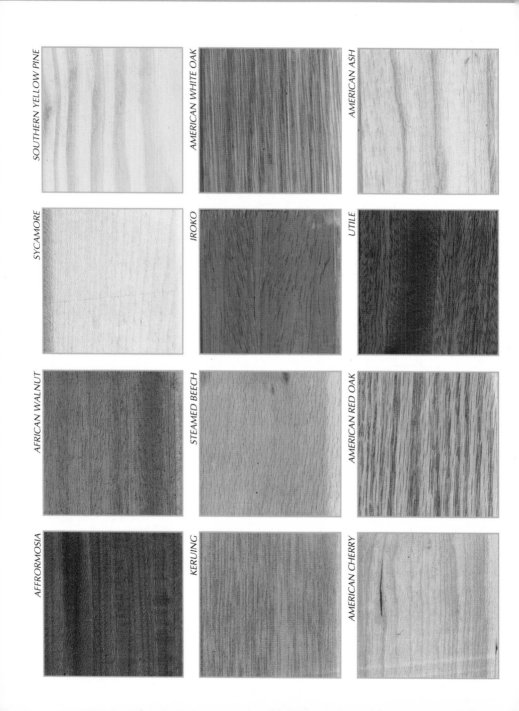

SOUTHERN YELLOW PINE

AMERICAN WHITE OAK

AMERICAN ASH

SYCAMORE

IROKO

UTILE

AFRICAN WALNUT

STEAMED BEECH

AMERICAN RED OAK

AFFRORMOSIA

KERUING

AMERICAN CHERRY

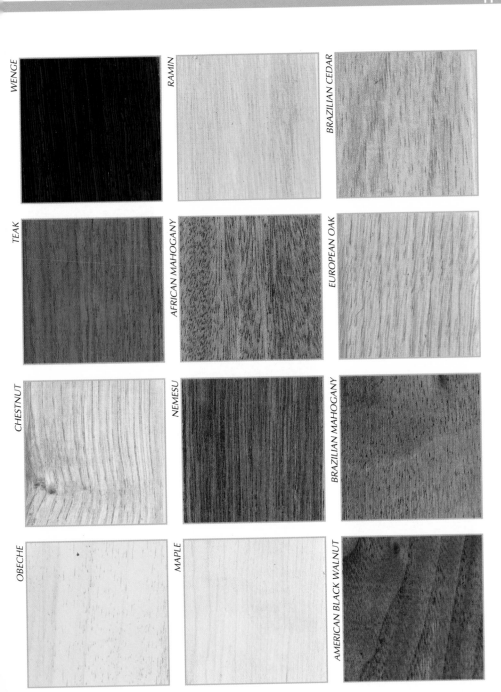

WENGE

RAMIN

BRAZILIAN CEDAR

TEAK

AFRICAN MAHOGANY

EUROPEAN OAK

CHESTNUT

NEMESU

BRAZILIAN MAHOGANY

OBECHE

MAPLE

AMERICAN BLACK WALNUT

MAN-MADE BOARDS

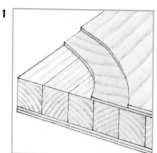

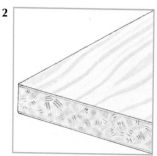

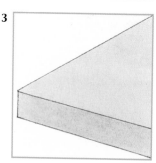

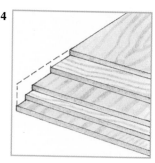

Apart from their cheapness, there are two advantages to buying man-made boards rather than 'natural' timber.
The first is that they are supplied in a larger size than the real thing – 2440mmx1220mm/8ftx4ft is a standard sheet size. The second is that they can be stronger than real timber by virtue of the fact that the different layers of the board use wood with the grain running in different directions.

1   BLOCKBOARD – has one grain direction for the central strips and the opposite grain direction for the surface veneers. Wood bends more, but breaks less along the grain than across it.

2   CHIPBOARD – is one of the cheapest man-made boards and consists of wood chippings held together with glue. It is widely used in kitchen unit and cheaper furniture construction, especially when faced with melamine or covered with a hardwood veneer. Although not very strong (except flooring grades), chipboard is a versatile and popular material; its biggest disadvantages are that it weakens considerably if subjected to moisture and is very hard work to cut because of the glue, wearing out saws fairly rapidly. It does not take ordinary wood-screws very well.

3   MEDIUM-DENSITY FIBREBOARD – is a recent development. Made from wood fibres bonded together, it has several advantages over chipboard which it is largely replacing, especially for things like fitted bedroom furniture. For a start, it is easier to cut and has a much smoother surface, it takes paint well and will take ordinary wood screws without splitting.

4   PLYWOOD – which has attractive facing veneers, has several thin sheets with the grain running at right angles in alternate layers.

MOULDINGS

As well as buying timber with square edges, you can buy a wide variety of mouldings where a square-edged piece of timber has a profile shaped by a machine.

Apart from the huge range of specialist mouldings available for picture framing – mainly from art shops and specialist suppliers – most of the mouldings you will come across are used for constructional detailing in and around the home.

One of the most familiar is the plain shaped moulding or more ornate 'ogee' moulding used for architraves – the framing around door openings. Plain or more ornate mouldings are similarly used for skirtings and cornices. Decorative mouldings may also be used for picture rails and dado rails.

In glazed doors and in some windows, glazing bead is used to hold the glass in place; a moulded weatherbar is used on the outside of external doors to throw the rain off.

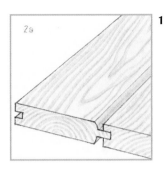

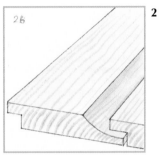

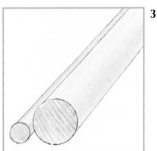

1   MATCHING – is a tongue-and-groove timber cladding. It can be for interior or exterior use.

2   SHIPLAP – is a timber cladding with one scalloped edge. It can be for interior or exterior use.

For woodworkers, a whole range of small mouldings are available, including square, triangular, half-round, quarter-round (quadrant) and circular shapes.

3   CIRCULAR MOULDING – is often known as doweling as it can be cut up into short lengths to be used in dowel joints or for reinforcing other kinds of joints.

4   LIPPINGS – are small hardwood mouldings often used to provide an attractive edge to blockboard shelving.

ADHESIVES AND FILLERS

M ost woodworking joints are reinforced with adhesive. The type of adhesive you should use depends on the components being jointed and where they are to be used.

The most common and widely available woodworking adhesive is PVA – polyvinyl acetate adhesive. This white creamy liquid is applied to both surfaces to be joined which must be clamped while the adhesive sets. Excess adhesive can be removed with a damp cloth before it dries, or once set, it is colourless and can be picked off with a sharp knife.

If a PVA adhesive is used, the joint is made for life. There are waterproof adhesives for outdoor use that are available from do-it-yourself stores or from timber merchants.

For furniture restoration, natural glues, mainly fish and animal glues or 'Scotch' glue are used. These have to be heated, but their big advantage is that the glue can be softened by applying wet heat allowing the furniture to be taken apart. Natural glues are more difficult to find and are mainly available from specialist suppliers.

Using screws for joining wood can leave the screw heads exposed or some joints may not be perfect leaving exposed gaps. A filler is useful to solve both these problems.

Normal decorator's filler can be used if the surface is to be painted, but for large cracks it will not expand and contract with the natural movement of the wood. A wood stopper is a better choice – especially if the surface is to be stained or varnished or otherwise left looking 'natural'. Wood stoppers are available in a range of natural wood colours that can be mixed together or with a small amount of stain, to ensure a perfect match with the wood you are working on. Waterproof versions are available for outside use.

BELOW: A selection of ready-made cladding and mouldings.

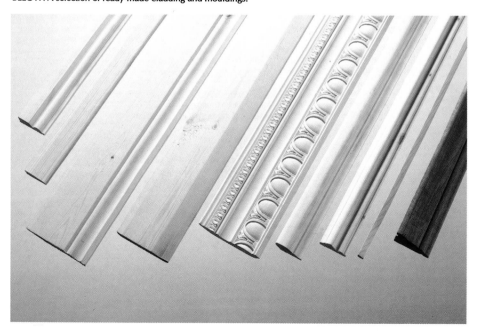

Made Simple
TOOLS, EQUIPMENT
AND TECHNIQUES

A variety of tools that are well maintained and sharp are essential to make quality joints.

1: COMBINATION SQUARE – provides both a 45° as well as a 90° setting angle and the steel 300mm/12in ruler it incorporates can be removed for separate use.

2: DIVIDERS – useful for transferring the measurement on one piece of wood to another and a home-made compass is useful for drawing circles.

3: MARKING GAUGE – for making a line a set distance from an edge, using the hardened pin on the adjustable stem while the stock is held against the edge of the wood.

4: MARKING KNIFE – for accurate lines, though the line is difficult to see in poor light.

5: PLUMBLINE – a weight on a length of cord or string, used for marking verticals.

6: RIGID RULE – either wooden or steel up to 1m/39in long or a folding wooden rule up to 914mm/36in long. Used for drawing straight lines.

7: SLIDING BEVEL – has a thin steel blade in a wooden handle and secured in place with a wing nut, used to set out angles other than 45° or 90°.

8: SPIRIT LEVEL – the longer the surface, the larger the level should be. If it is metal it can also be used as a straight-edge.

9: TAPE MEASURE – a 2m/6½ft steel is the minimum, but for larger frames, 3m/10ft or 5m/16ft tape is better. The type with a lock and marked in inches and millimetre is best.

10: TRY SQUARE – for marking cutting lines at right angles to a piece of wood. Used for checking external right angles after cutting or planing, and internal right angles when assembling frames or bookshelves.

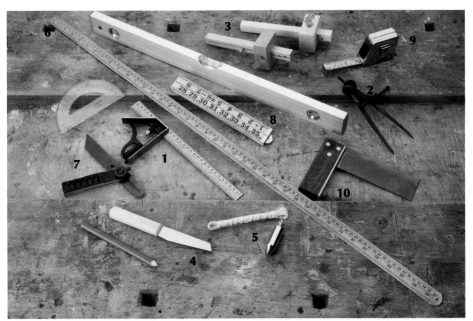

CUTTING WOOD

1: COPING SAW OR FRET SAW – used to cut curves in wood, both are pulled through the wood to cut on the back stroke rather than being pushed through the wood to cut on the forward stroke.
A JIGSAW – has short or long reach removable blades that can be set at an angle, or to suit different materials. It is the powered equivalent of the coping saw and the padsaw.

2: PADSAW OR KEYHOLE SAW – used to enlarge a hole in a piece of wood, or to cut out a piece from the centre of a board or panel.

3: PANEL SAW – around 500mm/20in long with about 9 teeth per inch. This can be used for cross-cutting – cutting across the grain, or for rip sawing – cutting along the grain. It is suitable for cutting man-made boards. To avoid the need for resharpening and resetting the saw, choose one with hardpoint teeth especially if you are cutting a lot of chipboard. Some people prefer traditional wooden handles whilst others are happier with modern plastic handles, some of which have 45° and 90° angles on their faces which can be used with the back of the saw as a rule for marking out timber.
A CIRCULAR SAW – is the powered equivalent of the panel saw, which can be set to cut at an angle or at a fixed distance from an edge and to cut at different depths.

4: TENON SAW – around 200mm/10in long with around 15 teeth to the inch – used for cutting joints. This is part of the 'backsaw' family, so called because the blade has a rigid steel spine or back running along the top to keep the blade straight. You cannot use a tenon saw for cutting through large pieces of wood as the back will get in the way, but it is the ideal tool to use for accurate cutting of joints.

USING A SAW

The golden rule when using any saw is to cut on the waste side of the line – always mark the waste side.

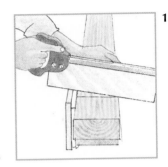

Panel saw or tenon saw

1 Point your index finger down the blade and use the full length of the blade.

2 Start the cut by drawing the blade back towards you held against the side of your thumb for accuracy.

3 If you wander off line with a panel saw, twist the blade to bring it back to line. With a tenon saw which is used at a less steep angle, start the cut again if you wander off line.

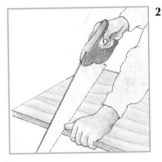

Coping saw or fret saw

4 A coping saw is used with the wood held vertically, the handle being screwed, is adjustable for both tension and position of the hooped back frame during cutting.

5 A fret saw should be held vertically with the handle below the timber pulling down on the cutting stroke, with the work positioned horizontally. This way you can see the line you should be following more clearly and you have more control.

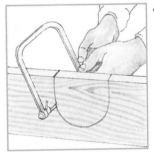

Padsaw or keyhole saw

7 Mark the outline of the shape you want to cut, then drill holes on the perimeter where the direction changes.

8 Keeping the handle horizontal, place the blade through one of the holes and cut on the push stroke.

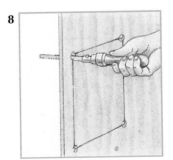

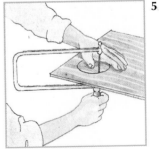

SHAPING WOOD

To shape wood you will need a selection of chisels.

1: BEVEL-EDGE CHISEL – is the most useful type. Available in a range of sizes from 6mm/1⁄4in to 38mm/11⁄2in, but what makes it useful is that is has sloping sides (bevels) on the top of the blade. These bevels allow the tool to be used for undercutting – that is cleaning out a corner of less than 90°, which is essential when making dovetail joints. It is useful to have around four different sizes of chisel.

2: FIRMER CHISEL – has a rectangular cross-section and is stronger than a bevel-edge chisel, which makes it more suitable for use when making mortice joints where the chisel is used to lever out the waste wood from a deep slot. You probably need only one or two sizes of firmer chisel – say 6mm/1⁄4in and 12mm/1⁄2in.

3: MORTICE CHISELS – which are even thicker and stronger than firmer chisels, but these are probably too specialised for most amateur woodworkers.

4: GOUGE – at least one gouge is helpful – this is a chisel with a curved blade and comes in two types (scribing and firmer) depending on whether it is being used on the concave inside surface of a curve or the convex outside surface.

USING A CHISEL

A chisel is used in four ways – for undercutting, for paring, for chopping and for morticing.

1 UNDERCUTTING – this is cleaning out a corner with an angle of less than 90°, an example is the angles when making dovetail joints.

2 PARING – is removing thin slivers of wood, it is best to use the chisel downwards using only enough hand pressure to slide it across the surface of the wood removing a thin sliver – place the work piece on a block of scrap wood so that you do not damage the work surface.

Keep the flat side of the blade towards the work.

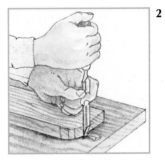

3 CHOPPING – this is removing larger amounts of wood – hit the end of the chisel handle with a mallet to force it through the wood. Face the flat side of the blade away from the work with the front bevel facing the work – this will prevent the chisel digging in and help to keep it on line.

4 MORTICING – cutting a slot for a mortice-and-tenon joint – first, the chisel is used for chopping (A) and then used as a lever (B) to remove the cut wood from the slot. The slot may already have been made using a drill (see page 37).

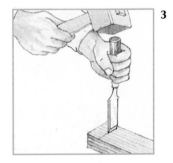

1

2

3

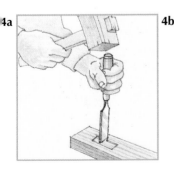

4a

4b

SMOOTHING WOOD

For giving cut surfaces a smooth finish you need a plane.

1: BLOCK PLANE – which is a small tool, with the plane blade set at a low angle, and is also used for trimming across the end grain of wood – something you can do much more accurately with this tool than with a chisel.
2: SMOOTHING PLANE – is used for giving smooth surfaces to lengths of timber. If you are making joints, you will also be involved in woodworking so a smoothing plane which is around 200-250mm/8-10in long will be useful.
3: ELECTRICAL PLANES – make removing wood quicker and easier especially when dressing (smoothing) lengths of timber to face-side and face-edge (squaring the surfaces) for stock. They are difficult to control because of the inertia created by the spinning blades. For this reason they are not suitable for accurate work and make a mess unless used with a vacuum cleaner adaptor.

USING A PLANE

It is vital that a plane blade is properly sharpened and is properly set – that is with just a small amount showing beneath the sole plate and with the blade parallel to the sole plate.

3

1 Set the projection of the blade to equal the depth of cut – the smaller the projection, the finer the finish.

2 The workpiece must be held securely in a bench or vice and the plane held firmly with both hands.

Using a smoothing plane

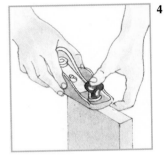

4

3 Try to work along the workpiece in a single stroke – at the start of the stroke have most weight on the hand holding the front of the plane (the left hand for right-handers) and gradually transfer the weight to the other hand.

Using a block plane

4 Used in its own unique way with the blade set to give a very fine cut. Always work from the outer edges of the work towards the centre – working towards the edge will split the wood – use small strokes rather like using a chisel.

DRILLING WOOD

For making small holes in wood up to around 9mm/³⁄8in, an electric drill or, if you prefer, a hand drill can be used with normal twist drill bits.

When using an electric drill for making holes, it is much better if this can be mounted in a drill stand with the work supported underneath. This way, you have a much better chance of getting the hole drilled straight and square and you can control the depth more accurately especially if the drill stand is fitted with a depth stop.

For making larger holes, 'spade' bits can be used with the electric drill or 'auger' bits used with a hand-operated brace. A brace-and-bit will give a more accurate hole, which may be essential when using large doweling rod of say 12mm/½in diameter.

Note that neither spade bits nor auger bits can be used to enlarge an existing hole. If a large hole is too small, you will have to use a round file or a gouge to make it bigger.

For smaller doweling, special drills bits are available which have a pronounced point and are easier to position. These come with rubber rings on them to act as depth stops and come in the three common dowel sizes – 6mm/¼in, 8mm/⁵16in and 10mm/³8in.

BELOW: A vertical stand attachment for a drill fitted with a depth stop is an extremely accurate tool.

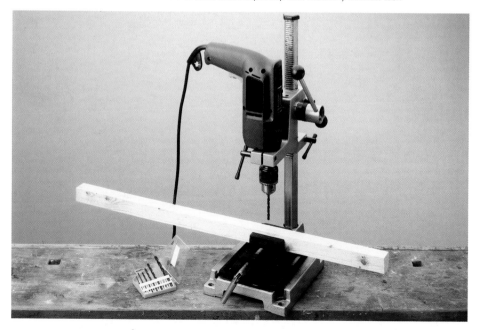

CUTTING MITRES AND ANGLES

Use a mitre-box – a three-sided U-shaped box with slots cut in the long sides.

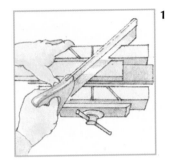

Accuracy is imperative when cutting mitres. One degree out, will cause a gap at either the inner or outer corner of the mitre, and if the cut is not straight, the two mouldings will not meet along their length.

1 Place the moulding inside the U resting on a scrap piece of wood, put a saw into a pair of slots to guide the saw at the correct angle through the wood.

Most mitre-boxes have three sets of slots – one for each 45° angle and one to cut through the moulding at 90°. A mitre block has only two sides and one slot to guide the saw.

It is worth investing in a mitre saw for cutting a lot of mitres for picture framing. This has a saw with a thin blade, which is held at an angle over a machined bed on which the moulding sits. It will accurately cut 45° and 90° angles, and can also be used for other angles.

WORKBENCH, VICES AND CLAMPS

When cutting or shaping wood, it is important that it is held securely.

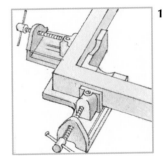

A workbench is essential to rest the workpiece on: a vice can be used to secure wood when planing, chiselling, sawing or drilling. Make sure it is a woodworking vice with large protected jaws; the serrated jaws of a metalworking vice will damage the surface of the wood.

A selection of clamps are needed for holding joints together while adhesive dries. Traditional G-clamps are the most useful, but larger sash clamps – or tape clamps – are needed for working on doors, windows and book-shelves.

1 One particularly useful clamp is a corner clamp which holds two pieces of wood at right angles but does not force them together. Some corner clamps have a slot which can be used for cutting a mitre.

NEXT PAGE: Objects made from wood have an irresistible appeal that causes them to become possessions.

Made Simple
WOODWORKING
JOINTS

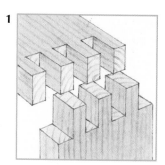

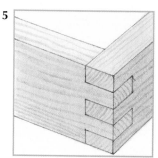

BOX JOINTS

A box or comb joint is used in furniture making for the corners of wide frames, boxes and drawers.

The two pieces of wood to be joined must be the same width and, preferably, the same thickness.

This joint performs much the same function as a dovetail joint, but is easier to make. It provides a greater gluing area than many other joints and if well made, looks good.

To make a corner L-box joint

1 Measure the width of wood being joined and divide it into an odd number to give alternate tenons and recesses of equal sizes so that the tenons in one piece fit into the recesses of the other.

The minimum width of a tenon is normally 10mm/^{3}8in – any less than this and the joint will be weakened.

2 Mark out all the tenons to the 'depth line' (the thickness of the wood) and use a pencil to cross-hatch the recesses so that you remember to cut on the waste side of each line.

3 Hold the wood vertically in the vice to cut down the lines with a tenon saw.

4 Use a chisel to chip out the waste wood, working from both sides towards the centre.

5 Use adhesive to assemble the joint, wipe off excess adhesive with a damp cloth and clamp the two pieces of wood at right angles while the glue sets.

To make a T-box joint

This is, in effect, a mortice-and-tenon joint with more than one tenon. To conceal the joint when making cabinets, for example, cut the tenons to half the thickness of the wood and make the mortices to half the depth to provide a 'stopped' joint.

1 Cut the tenons on the end of one piece of wood in the same way as above.

2 Cut the recesses (mortices) to marked positions on the other piece by drilling holes right through the wood.

3 Chop out the drilled holes to the edges of the marked positions using a chisel.

BRIDLE JOINTS

A bridle joint is used for joining pieces of wood of the same thickness and is useful when joining one long piece to the tops of several vertical pieces.

It is a strong joint, similar in many ways to the mortice-and-tenon joint. The rule for making a bridle joint is that the tenon should not be less than one quarter nor more than one-third of the thickness of the timber in which it is cut.

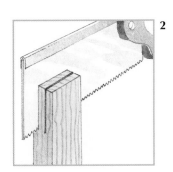

To make a corner bridle joint

1 Mark out the tenon and the tongues which form the slot using a mortice gauge – make the depth of the slot and the length of the tenon both slightly longer than the width of wood being joined.

2 Use a tenon saw to cut out the waste wood either side of the tenon and down the inner sides of the slot.

3 For the tenon, make two further cuts at the marked depth for the slot, and chip out the waste wood using a narrow chisel working from both sides towards the centre.

4 Assemble the joint using adhesive and use a block plane to remove the ends of the tongues and the end of the tenon once the adhesive has dried.

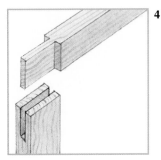

To make a T-bridle joint

5 Mark out the tenon and the tongues which fill the slot as described above in 1 and 2.

6 Cut down to the marked lines on either side of the tenon then chisel out the waste.

You will find it easier to make several more cuts down to the marked line before using a wide chisel, working from both outer sides towards the centre.

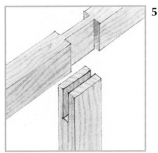

Make sure the gap you leave is exactly the width of the wood being used.

7 When the joint is assembled and the glue has dried, plane off the ends of the protruding tongues.

BUTT JOINTS

1

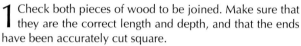

This is the simplest of all woodworking joints and only involves cutting the two pieces of wood to be joined so that they are the correct length and square.

Butt joints can be T-joints or L-joints and are used in making frames, such as those used in partition walls.

1 Check both pieces of wood to be joined. Make sure that they are the correct length and depth, and that the ends have been accurately cut square.

2 Make sure that the two surfaces to be joined are clean and free of grease. Apply glue to both surfaces.

3 Butt the pieces of wood together and secure them into position using the following options for reinforcement.

Reinforcement options

4

4 Screws are normally put through the joint; when using nails – angle them for greater strength (skew nailing).

5 T-shaped or L-shaped metal bracket can be unsightly – or use shaped blocks glued and pinned into the corners of the joint.

6 Sometimes a better option is to use a triangular shaped piece of plywood screwed over the joint.

7 For very light frames, corrugated fasteners or timber connectors can be used.

5

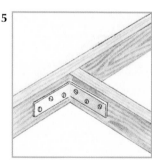

6

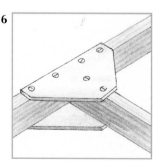

DOVETAIL JOINT

The dovetail joint is one of the most difficult to make, but is a challenge and, if well made, looks very attractive.

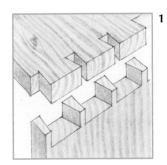

It comes in many guises, the most common of which is the through dovetail joint, which is used at the corners of boxes and drawers in much the same way as an L-box joint.

The strength of the dovetail joint comes from angled pins fitted into similarly angled recesses between larger tails. The pins are typically angled at 80° (1:6) for hardwood and 83° (1:8) for softwood and at their widest point are normally two-thirds the width of the tail at its narrowest point, but should not normally be less than 10mm/$\frac{3}{8}$in wide.

A dovetail joint can be used to join wood of different thicknesses – the pins should be in the thicker piece and the tails in the thinner piece.

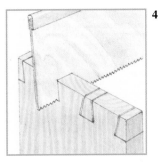

To mark out the tails

1 Decide how many tails you are going to have and then divide the width of the wood by that number.

Divide this answer by five to give an answer x. The tails are then 3x at their narrowest point (the shoulder) and the recesses for the pins are 2x at their widest point – the half recesses at either edge are x wide.

2 Butt the two pieces of wood together and mark lines on each piece to represent the thickness of the other.

3 Mark out the tails on one of the two pieces (the thinner one if they are unequal).

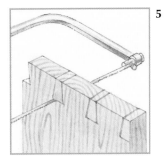

You can use a sliding bevel set to 80° or 83° to mark the angles of the dovetails (mark half the lines before turning it over) or you could make yourself a small mortice gauge out of a piece of thin metal sheet.

4 Once the tails have all been marked (with the recesses for the pins cross-hatched), cut down the waste sides of the lines using a tenon saw.

5 Use a coping saw, carefully insert the blade to cut along the bottom of the recess.

6 Use a bevel-edge chisel to clean out the corners. If you are making four repeat corners for a box, align the two opposite sides, then nail them together before clamping them in a vice. Cut the tails in both pieces at the same time.

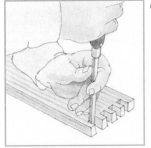

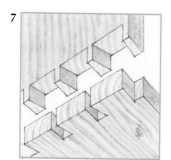

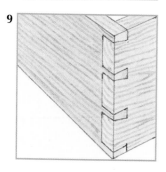

To mark out the pins

7 Use the cut tails as an accurate guide for marking out the pins – use a marking knife to mark precise cut-lines.

8 Cut out the pins in the same way as for the tails and try the joint for fit.

The joint should be a tight fit, needing a mallet (or hammer and scrap wood) to drive it home – if it is too tight, use a chisel to remove some slivers of wood – if it too loose, use some slivers as packing.

9 Apply woodworking adhesive to the joint surfaces, re-assemble and clamp it up square while the adhesive sets.
    The two pieces of wood cannot be pulled apart once the joint is made.

When making a box or a drawer, assemble all the corners at the same time.

DOWEL JOINTS

A dowel joint is basically a butt joint reinforced with 6mm, 8mm or 10mm dowels.

Both the pieces of wood to be joined have drilled holes into which the dowels fit. The secret of making this joint is to ensure the holes line up and that the two wood surfaces mate accurately.

A proper doweling drill bit should be used – this has a sharp centre point making it easier to position and comes with a rubber ring to use as a depth gauge.

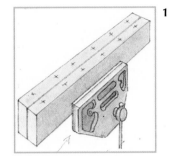

Secret dowel joints

These are extremely good for joining pieces of wood end to end or edge to edge. The dowels are completely hidden but this form of joint is difficult to make. There are three options for ensuring the holes are in the correct place:

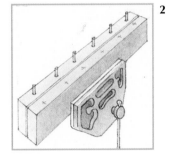

1 Mark out the holes with both bits of wood clamped together, making sure they are exactly in the middle of the thickness and then drill them out making sure the drill is square to the doweled edge.

2 Make the holes in one piece, then fit 'centre points' into the holes and use these to mark the position of the holes in the other piece – drill these out as before.

3 Use a doweling 'jig' which will also help to guide the drill bit square to the wood.

4 Once the holes have been made, put a little adhesive into each hole and tap the dowels into place.

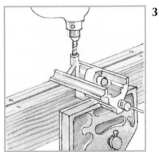

If you use dowel cut from a rod, make one or more grooves along the length so that the glue can escape from the hole – pre-cut dowels are fluted to allow this.

To make a through dowel joint (used at corners)

5 Cut the two pieces to be joined to the correct size and then clamp in their final position.

6 Use a dowel bit to drill holes right through one piece of wood into the other.

7 Apply wood adhesive to the holes and insert the dowel. Leave a bit of the dowel protruding so that it can be cut flush with the wood once the adhesive has dried.

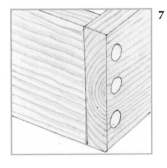

HALVING JOINTS

1

Although not very strong, the halving or half-lap joint is useful for making frames and other carpentry jobs.

It is made by cutting out each piece of wood to half its thickness (it is used only when joining two bits of wood of the same thickness) and then joining them together.

To make a corner halving joint

2

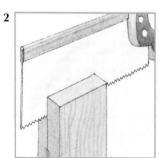

1 Slightly overlap the two pieces of wood to be joined and mark the width and position on each piece. The excess can be removed once the joint is made.

2 Cut down the grain at an angle from both sides before finishing by cutting square.

3 Cut accurately across the grain to remove the waste part of the joint.

4 Repeat the process for the second piece of wood. Then apply the adhesive and clamp into position until set.

3

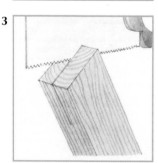

4

Variations

The following variations are made using a similar method as for making a corner halving joint.

5 T-HALVING – is made in a similar way, except that for one of the pieces of wood you need to chisel out the recess.

6 DOVETAIL HALVING – the joint is shaped like a dovetail, thus preventing the two pieces being pulled apart.

7 CROSS HALVING – two bits of wood cross-over without increasing the thickness of the frame. Both recesses need to be cut and chiselled out of both pieces of wood.

8 LAP JOINT – is used on wood of different thicknesses. It is used in much the same way as a halving joint, but the recess in one piece of wood is cut to a depth equal to the whole thickness of the inset piece.

5

6   7   8

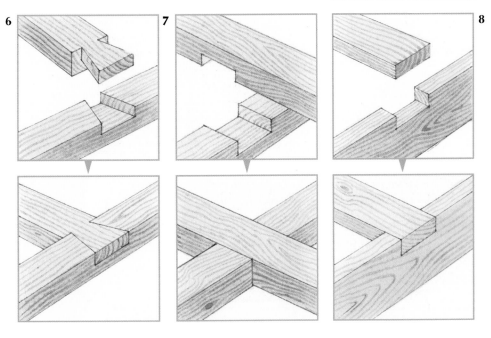

HOUSING JOINTS

1

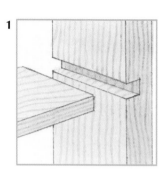

3

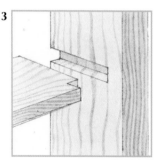

5

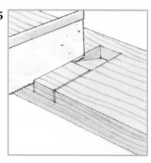

6

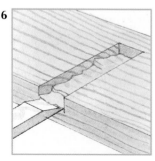

A housing joint is used for making bookcases where shelves are supported by side uprights.

A slot is cut out of the uprights and a shelf is fitted into it. Where the bookcase is free-standing, the joint needs to be reinforced with adhesive; where the uprights are restrained (as in an alcove), the joint can be left unglued if you want to be able to remove the shelves.

To make a through housing joint

1 Mark the thickness of the cross member – make sure that it is in the correct position and square on the upright.

2 Use a tenon saw to cut to the depth of the recess, then remove the waste with a chisel.

A router, guided along a timber batten clamped to the workpiece can be used to cut the slot. The router can be set to give a slot of exactly the correct depth – no more than half the thickness of the upright – one or two passes can be made depending on the thickness of cutter used relative to the width of slot required.

To make a stopped housing joint

3 Mark the thickness of the cross member – make sure that it is in the correct position and square-on to the upright.

4 Mark off 20mm/¾in of the slot short of the front edge on the upright – do not remove this.

5 Use a tenon saw to carefully cut on the waste side to the depth of the recess.

6 Then remove the waste from the recess with a chisel and square off the front stop of the housing.

If a router is used, you will need to square off the stopped end of the slot with a chisel.

7 Cut a matching 20mm/¾in piece from the front edge of the cross member so that the final effect is that of a simple butt joint.

KNOCKDOWN JOINTS

Although not woodworking joints as such, 'knock-down' fittings are widely used in modern flat-pack furniture to join timber and, especially, man-made boards together.

Normally, minimal cutting of the timber or board is needed, though some fittings require a hole to take screws.

Common types of knock-down fittings

1 CHIPBOARD SCREWS – have a thread which bites into the chipboard, often used for joining cupboards together.

2 CHIPBOARD PLUGS – used in the same way as a wallplug to take a normal wood screw.

3 BLOCK JOINTS – used to join two boards at right angles – a two-piece block is easier to take apart than a one-piece.

4 CAM JOINTS – are used at corners, but do not take up any room inside the cupboard. They need holes to be drilled into the boards to take the two halves of the joint.

5 PANEL BUTT JOINT CONNECTORS – join two lengths of board (typically worktops) end to end.

6 CABINET CONNECTING SCREWS – used to hold adjoining cabinets together.

For making the flat-bottomed recess to take a cam joint or a panel butt joint connector – for cupboard hinges – you need a special type of drill bit called an 'end mill'. This has a flat tip to make a flat-bottomed hole and is best used in an electric drill fitted in a drill stand with a depth stop.

LAP JOINTS – See halving joints.

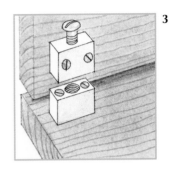

3

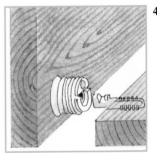

4

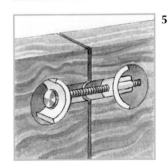

5

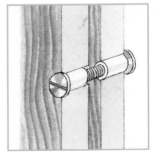

6

MITRE JOINT

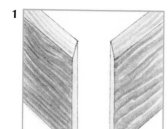

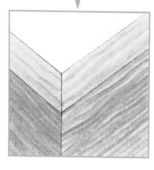

1

This joint has two main uses. The first is specifically for making picture frames, the second is for neat corners when fitting architrave moulding around door frames.

1 Mark the cutting angle of 45° on the top edges of both the pieces to be joined. When they are put together, they should make an exact right angle.

2 Use a try square to mark the saw guide lines on either side of each of the pieces of wood.

3 Using a tenon saw cut the mitres on both pieces of wood – the mitre can be cut freehand; using either a mitre block or box; or using a mitre saw (see page 23).

4 Either, nail from the outside of the corner through the mitre and into the width of the timber.

Or, apply adhesive to both surfaces and then cramp into position. Remove excess adhesive, and leave to dry.

Although the joint looks good – because no end grain is exposed – it is very weak unless reinforced in some way.

MORTICE-AND-TENON-JOINT

A mortice-and-tenon joint is one of the strongest used by woodworkers. It is used widely in doors and windows and in making frames.

A mortice-and-tenon joint can be used either at a corner where a top or bottom rail meets a side rail or to make a T-joint, where a centre rail meets a side rail.

In all cases, the joint consists of a tongue (the tenon) which fits into a matching hole (the mortice).

The joint can either be 'stopped' – the tenon cannot be seen – or 'through' – the mortice passes through the wood.

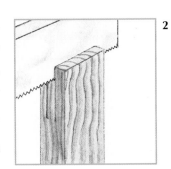

2

To cut the tenon

For a stopped joint, the tenon should be a little shorter than the depth of the hole; for a through joint, it should be a little longer than the width of the wood, so it can be trimmed off.

1 Mark up the piece of wood so that the tenon is the full width of the wood but only one third of the thickness.

2 First use a tenon saw to cut down the grain, then across the grain to remove both the outside thirds of the wood.

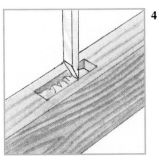

4

To cut the mortice

3 Accurately mark up the mortice in the correct position for the centre one third of the thickness of the wood.

4 Use a firmer or mortice chisel to dig out the wood and square off the edges. The joint needs to be a tight fit, so you should check the fit regularly at this stage.

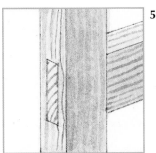

5

To speed things up – use a drill to remove the centre waste.

5 Apply adhesive to both mortice and tenon – cramp the assembly, remove excess glue and leave to set.

6 Strengthen the joint using dowels at right angles through the tongue (a good way of reinforcing old loose joints).

7 Or use wedges driven-in from the end either side of the tenon. With a through joint, the edges of the mortice need to be tapered to allow for these. With a stopped joint, the wedges are inserted into saw cuts on the tenon.

7

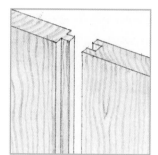

TONGUE-AND-GROOVE JOINT

Tongue-and-groove joints are used mainly on timber cladding and on flooring where one piece of timber is put in place tight up against another.

Both the tongues and the grooves are already cut – the tongue on one side and the groove on the other.

All you have to do is to assemble the boards correctly so that the tongue on one piece fits neatly into the groove on the next.

For cladding

The tongues are not pushed fully home into the groove – a small gap should be left for expansion.

For flooring

It is essential that the boards are pulled as tight together as possible. Sheet chipboard flooring and timber floor-covering have tongue-and-groove on the ends of the board as well as along the edge.

RIGHT: Flat or curved surfaces – all are made using joints. Can you find a joint that you recognise in this photograph?

Elizabeth Whiting Associates

Made Simple
USING WOOD-
WORKING JOINTS

It is all very well knowing what all the joints are called and how to make them. In practice, as with all jobs around the home, it is knowing which is the best joint to use for which job.

BELOW: A well crafted and attractive entrance hall that is both functional and stylish, yet pleasantly inviting.

Elizabeth Whiting Associates

MAKING A DRAWER

If you are making replacement drawers to fit into an old and, perhaps, valuable piece of furniture, you will want to make the joints in the same way as the original.

1 They will either be dovetail joints (see page 29) or box joints (see page 26). With both of these, the drawer front will usually be an integral part of the drawer and be jointed to the sides; sometimes, the drawer front will be fitted separately onto the front of a square-sided box.

2 When using dovetail joints to make a drawer, make sure the tails are on the side pieces facing forwards – these will prevent the drawer being pulled apart as it is yanked in and out. A lapped dovetail is often used for the front corners of the drawer so that the tails do not show. Here, the tails on the side pieces, and the recesses to take them, are cut to less than the thickness of the drawer front.

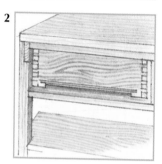

3 A very important part of the drawer is its base. In wooden furniture, this will usually be plywood, normally fitted into slots routed out of the front and sides and overlapping the back, so that it can be slid into place once the drawer is made and then secured by nailing up through the base into the back. Sometimes, the base will be supported by L-shaped pieces of timber glued to the sides.

With modern kitchen cupboards, do not use wooden drawers. Not only are they hard to make accurately, but they will get dirty rapidly and will tend to swell as the humidity in the kitchen varies.

4 Instead, you can buy drawer-making kits, which consist of lengths of pre-moulded plastic channelling which are joined together at the corners by plastic connectors. The base of the tray is melamine-faced hardboard, slid into a groove in the sides and back – note that this usually has to be put into place before the drawer is finally assembled. As with wooden drawers, there is a choice of having the drawer front as part of the drawer or of screwing it on to the front of a box structure. When replacing broken drawers, re-use the old drawer fronts.

MAKING A FRAME

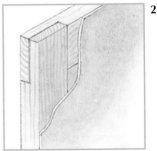

1

The type of joint(s) you should use when making up frames, depends on what the frame is to be used for, whether it will be seen and how big it is.

1 PARTITION WALL – The framework for a partition wall is made from 100mmx50mm/4inx2in rough-sawn timber. Simple butt joints (see page 28), reinforced with skew nails, can be used where the uprights (studs) meet the top and bottom rails of the frame and where the horizontal noggins meet the uprights. The frame itself will be secured in position (by nailing the sole plate and head plate to the floor and ceiling and screwing the end studs to the side walls), so there is little trying to pull the frame apart.

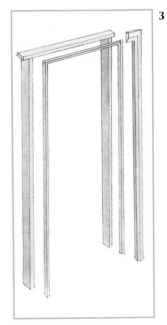

2

2 FLUSH DOOR – If you want to make a lightweight flush door to fit a particular size of hole, the framework can be made using simple halving joints (see page 32) secured with adhesive. The frame will be secured in place (and prevented from twisting) by the hardboard or other covering which you nail to both sides of the door frame. A stronger result would be achieved using bridle joints at the corners and where any horizontal frame members meet the side uprights.

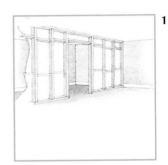

3

3 DOOR FRAMES – An internal door frame usually consists simply of three pieces of wood butt jointed together and screwed to the wall.

Once the frame is in place, a door stop is fitted and architrave added. For standard sizes of external door, with a sill, you can buy the door frame components already fitted with mortice-and-tenon joints and all you need to do is to fit them into the opening.

But if you need to make up a new frame for a non-standard door size, cut mortices at either end of the frame head and the sill to take tenons on the two side uprights (jambs) and assemble the frame before fitting it into the opening.

MAKING A BOOKCASE

1

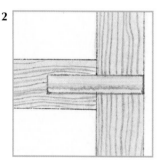

For a free-standing bookcase, you will want the joints between the shelves and the side uprights to look as neat as possible.

1 The simplest way to make a bookcase is to cut the shelves and the uprights to length and then to drill holes in the uprights and butt joint (see page 28) them to the uprights with reinforcing screws through the uprights into the ends of the shelves. This has the disadvantage that the screw heads will show, but you could conceal them by drilling the hole a little deeper (counterboring) so that the screw heads are below the surface and then use decorators filler if painting the bookcase or wood stopper if varnishing or staining it. An even neater result can be obtained by using a combination drill bit (which drills the pilot hole, clearance hole and counterbore for the screw in one go), plus a 'plug cutter' on a waste piece of the same wood to cut out a circular plug of exactly the correct size to go into the hole. Careful choice of whereabouts in the scrap wood you cut the hole and how you fit it into the hole can mean that you can very nearly match up the grain size and direction.

2

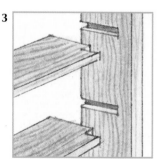

2 Another way to make a bookcase is to use doweled joints (see page 31) – stopped dowels, will look neater than through dowels – but these are really suitable only for bookcases taking a light load as heavy books could break the dowels.

3

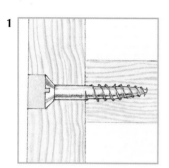

3 A stronger answer, but one which requires more skill and the use of a router, is to use a housing joint (see page 34) where the shelves fit into slots cut out of the uprights, either glued or screwed in place to strengthen the joint. For a neater result, use a stopped housing which looks like a butt joint, but is much stronger.

DOORS AND WINDOWS

It is unlikely that you will be making doors and windows to fit into your home – as ready-made doors and windows in both standard and non-standard sizes are available.

It is possible that you will need to repair a door or window where the glue in the joints has dried out and/or the wood has shrunk.

Most door and window joints are mortice-and-tenon joints (see page 37). Sometimes, it may be possible to squeeze more adhesive into the joint and simply clamp it up while the adhesive sets. But normally, the joint will need reinforcing in some way. If the joints have wedges, new and perhaps larger wedges can be cut from scrap timber and hammered into the joints along with some new adhesive, clamping up the joints while the adhesive dries and trimming off the excess wedge afterwards.

Joints without wedges can be reinforced by the use of dowels fitted across the joint – i.e. through holes drilled so that they pass right through the tenon. It is essential that the dowels glued into these holes are a good tight fit, so it is better to use doweling rod to effect the repair and choose a drill bit size so that the rod has to be tapped into the hole – experiment on some scrap timber before attacking the joint itself.

BELOW: With so many moving parts in doors and windows, they eventually need repairs to minor damage.

Elizabeth Whiting Associates

KITCHEN UNITS

2

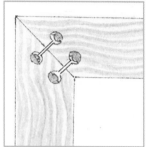

Most 'flat-pack' kitchen units come pre-drilled with holes to take chipboard screws or one of the other knock-down fittings (see page 35).

But you might need to modify a cupboard to fit a particular space or to re-drill holes which have been made incorrectly or to repair damaged kitchen units.

You might want to make your own kitchen cupboards if you have a particular space to fill or if there is nothing on the market which quite suits your needs. Study the section on knock-down fittings and look to see what is available in your local do-it-yourself store, before designing and making the kitchen units.

One task you may have to do yourself is to cut and fit worktops. These are usually available in 3m/9½ft lengths so it is unlikely that you will need to join two lengths together – but if you do, you can get jointing strips to do this or use the panel butt joint connectors described on page 35.

Joining worktops at corners

1 The simple way is to use a metal jointing strip which is shaped to fit the curved front edge of one length and the square-shaped edge of the other; a more complicated, but neater, way is to make a mitre joint.

2 This needs to be marked out and cut out extremely accurately and the joint is held together with panel butt joint connectors fitted across the joint and secured from underneath.

3 To fit these, make large round holes in the underneath of the worktop and then chisel a joining slot to take the connector bolt.

4 To prevent moisture getting into the joint, apply a wood-working adhesive to both faces before finally tightening the connectors and make certain that the two surfaces of the worktops being jointed are absolutely flush.

SKIRTINGS, CORNICES AND ARCHITRAVES

Aℓℓ these mouldings have a dual purpose – to cover up a gap in the house construction and to look decorative.

1 An architrave is fitted around internal door frames and in older houses, around window openings. The moulding is in three pieces – two for the sides and one across the top – joined with mitre joints (see page 36).

It is important that mitres are cut in straight lines, but they will rarely be 45°. Cut one half of the mitre at slightly more or slightly less than 45° as the door frame will not be exactly square. Cut the two side pieces first, then use these to mark the cutting lines for the top piece.

The architrave itself, which covers the gap between the door frame and the wall plaster, is nailed to the door frame. It is not necessary to glue the corners of an architrave, but nails are usually driven in downwards through the top piece into the side members to secure them in place.

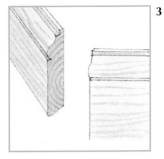

2 'Constructional' mouldings – skirtings, cornices, picture and dado rails are fitted around a room – skirtings to cover the gap between wall and floor and cornices to cover gaps between wall and ceiling.

Where skirtings and dado rails meet a door frame, they are cut square to butt up against the edge of the door frame. Where any of these mouldings meets another length of the same moulding – at the corner of a room – make a joint.

Square-edge skirtings are the easiest – cut them square to make a butt joint (see page 28), fitting one piece into the corner and overlap it with the second. The same technique is used on external corners.

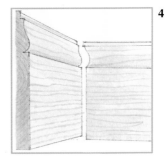

3 For moulded skirtings, dado and picture rails, you will have to use a different technique. At external corners, use a mitre joint (see page 36) and cut the skirting to go past the corner by the thickness of the board.

4 Using a mitre joint at internal corners is tricky if the room is not absolutely square and causes problems getting the final piece of moulding into place. A solution is to make a shaped butt joint where the end of one piece of moulding is cut to the profile of the other.

The first piece is cut square and put into the corner, the second piece is shaped and then fitted over it.

PANELLING AND FLOORCOVERING

Panelling goes on walls and floorcoverings go on floors, but their common feature is tongue-and-groove joints.

These are ready cut in the timber or board when bought but you have to ensure that the joints are made properly.

For panelling

1 The joints allow for expansion and contraction of the timber so the tongue of one piece is not pushed totally home into the groove of the next.

Each board is individually nailed or clipped into place.

For flooring

2 The floorboards, the chipboard flooring or the hardwood floorcovering must have as few gaps as possible so the joints are pushed home.

With 'floating' hardwood floors, the joints are glued so that expansion and contraction takes place at the edges of the floor by leaving a gap, covered with quadrant or scotia moulding.

Floorboard clamps can be hired. They clamp to the floor joists, and when pressure is applied will push the floorboards or chipboard sheets together.

An alternative is to hammer the boards together but make sure that you use some scrap wood – preferably a flooring offcut – to protect the exposed tongue.

Flooring is always started by facing a groove to the wall and the last lengths on the other side of the room are cut to fit the available gap.

Photography props supplied by:

Nina Barough Styling

Cover: Woodworking joints supplied by 3F Joiners

As credited, photographic material reproduced by kind permission of:

Elizabeth Whiting Associates